Enslow
PUBLISHING

WHO'S THE GRE

LIONEL MESSI VS. PELÉ

KATHLEEN CONNORS

SOCCER'S GREATEST

Please visit our website, www.enslow.com. For a free color catalog of all our high-quality books, call toll free 1-800-398-2504 or fax 1-877-980-4454.

Cataloging-in-Publication Data

Names: Connors, Kathleen.
Title: Lionel Messi vs. Pelé: soccer's greatest / Kathleen Connors.
Description: Buffalo, NY : Enslow Publishing, 2026. | Series: Who's the greatest?: sports stars | Includes glossary and index.
Identifiers: ISBN 9781978546981 (pbk.) | ISBN 9781978546998 (library bound) | ISBN 9781978547001 (ebook)
Subjects: LCSH: Messi, Lionel, 1987—Juvenile literature. | Pelé, 1940-2022–Juvenile literature. | Soccer players–Biography–Juvenile literature. | Soccer–Records–Juvenile literature.
Classification: LCC GV942.7.M398 C66 2026 | DDC 796.334092–dc23

Published in 2026 by
Enslow Publishing
2544 Clinton Street
Buffalo, NY 14224

Designer: Tanya Dellaccio Keeney
Editor: Kristen Rajzak Nelson and Therese Shea

Photo credits: Cover (Messi) Mark Pain/Alamy Images; cover (Pelé) PA Images/Alamy Images; p. 5 (Messi) Ringo Chiu/Shutterstock.com; p. 5 (Pelé) https://upload.wikimedia.org/wikipedia/commons/a/a9/Pele_con_brasil.jpg; p. 7 (Pelé) https://upload.wikimedia.org/wikipedia/commons/5/53/Pele_Netherlands_1962_%28cropped%29.jpg; p. 7 (map) Peter Hermes Furian/Shutterstock.com; p. 9 https://upload.wikimedia.org/wikipedia/commons/2/26/Leo_messi_barce_2005.jpg; p. 10 https://upload.wikimedia.org/wikipedia/commons/9/98/Pelé_1960.jpg; p. 11 mooinblack/Shutterstock.com; p. 13 https://upload.wikimedia.org/wikipedia/commons/6/6c/Brazil_1970.JPG; p. 15 Fabideciria/Shutterstock.com; p. 16 https://upload.wikimedia.org/wikipedia/commons/5/5a/PELÉ_-_1963_(cropped).jpg; p. 17 cristiano barni/Shutterstock.com; p. 18 https://upload.wikimedia.org/wikipedia/commons/0/0e/Italy_v_Brazil,_12_May_1963_-_Trapattoni_and_Pelé.jpg; p. 19 Debby Wong/Shutterstock.com; p. 20 https://upload.wikimedia.org/wikipedia/commons/c/c8/Pele_debut_v_tornado.jpg; pp. 21, 23 Christian Bertrand/Shutterstock.com; p. 24 https://upload.wikimedia.org/wikipedia/commons/6/66/Pelé_&_Lula.jpg; p. 25 Maciej Rogowski Photo/Shutterstock.com; p. 26 https://upload.wikimedia.org/wikipedia/commons/8/85/Pele_celebrating_1970.jpg; p. 27 ACHPF/Shutterstock.com; p. 29 (Pelé) A.RICARDO/Shutterstock.com; p. 29 (Messi) YES Market Media/Shutterstock.com.

Printed in the United States of America

CPSIA compliance information: Batch #CW26ENS: For further information contact Enslow Publishing, at 1-800-398-2504.

CONTENTS

Words in the glossary appear in **bold** type the first time they are used in the text.

SOCCER GOATS

How is greatness measured in the "beautiful game" of soccer? Is it the number of **career** goals scored? Or maybe the number of FIFA World Cup-winning teams a player was part of? Championships in a professional soccer **league** could be another measurement.

Pelé and Lionel Messi played at different times in the history of soccer. In some ways, that makes them hard to compare. Still, they're both in the running for the greatest soccer player of all time!

Did You Know?

In the United States, the sport of Pelé and Messi is called soccer. Elsewhere in the world, it may be called football or fútbol.

PELÉ

LIONEL MESSI

MESSI HAS WORN A FEW DIFFERENT JERSEY NUMBERS. TODAY, HE WEARS 10. PELÉ ALSO WORE NUMBER 10!

MEET PELÉ

The soccer great known as Pelé was born Edson Arantes do Nascimento on October 23, 1940, in Três Corações in southeastern Brazil. He grew up in Bauru in the Brazilian state of São Paulo. Pelé's father played minor league soccer when Pelé was growing up. Pelé began playing soccer at a young age.

Pelé played soccer in the streets near his home as a child. Then, in 1956, at age 16, he went to play for Santos Football Club.

Did You Know?

When Pelé was a child, Brazil lost in the World Cup. His father cried. So, Pelé promised to win the World Cup for his father!

SOCCER WAS A BIG PART OF PELÉ'S LIFE FROM THE START.

MEET MESSI

Lionel Andrés Messi Cuccitini was born on June 24, 1987, in Rosario, Argentina. He lived with his parents, Jorge and Celia. Messi has two brothers and one sister. When Messi began playing soccer as a kid, his dad coached the team.

In 1995, Messi joined a soccer team in Rosario called Newell's Old Boys. His talent for the sport was spotted by soccer teams all over the world. When Messi was just 13, he and his family moved to Barcelona, Spain, for him to play soccer.

Did You Know?

Friends and family call Messi "Leo."

ONCE IN BARCELONA, YOUNG MESSI PLAYED FOR FC BARCELONA'S TEAM FOR PLAYERS UNDER 14.

YOUNG STARS

With Santos, Pelé won nine league championships in São Paulo. He also played for the Brazilian national team. By the mid-1960s, Pelé was a hero to Brazilians. They called him "Pérola Negra," or the "Black Pearl."

PELÉ PLAYED INSIDE LEFT FORWARD.

Did You Know?

FC Barcelona plays in La Liga as well as taking part in the Champions League, a top soccer league for European teams.

Messi began playing for FC Barcelona in 2004. He was just 17 years old! In La Liga, the highest league in Spain, Messi was the youngest player overall and the youngest player to score a goal.

IN MESSI'S SECOND SEASON WITH FC BARCELONA (2005–2006), THE TEAM WON THE CHAMPIONS LEAGUE TITLE.

WORLD CUPS

Heading into the 1958 World Cup, Pelé had a knee injury. He was just 17 too. The coach of the Brazilian national team wasn't sure he wanted Pelé to play. Still, when the team reached the World Cup finals in Sweden, Pelé played, getting an assist in the first game.

Pelé scored a hat trick—three goals in one game—against France in the semifinal. He scored two more goals in the final game. Brazil won! The Brazilian government named Pelé a national treasure for his play.

Did You Know?

The best player in the World Cup **tournament** is awarded the Golden Ball.

THREE WORLD CUP WINS (1958, 1962, 1970)

WINNER OF THE GOLDEN BALL (1970)

PELÉ PLAYED FOR BRAZIL'S NATIONAL TEAM IN THE 1966 WORLD CUP BUT THE TEAM DIDN'T MAKE IT FAR IN THE TOURNAMENT. IN A TOTAL OF 14 WORLD CUP GAMES, OR MATCHES, PELÉ SCORED 12 GOALS.

Even though Messi is one of the greatest soccer players of all time, he didn't win a World Cup final until many years into his career. As of 2025, Messi has played for Argentina's national team in the World Cup five times, in 2006, 2010, 2014, 2018, and 2022.

In 2022, Messi and the Argentine national team faced France in the World Cup finals in Qatar. Messi scored two goals as well as scored during the final shootout to beat the French team.

Did You Know?

As of 2025, Messi is the only two-time winner of the Golden Ball.

WORLD CUP WINNER (2022)

TWO-TIME WINNER OF THE WORLD CUP'S GOLDEN BALL (2014, 2022)

RECORD FOR MOST MINUTES PLAYED IN WORLD CUP GAMES (2,314)*
*AS OF 2025

MESSI PLAYED IN THE WORLD CUP TOURNAMENT AS A TEENAGER, IN HIS 20S, AND IN HIS 30S. HE'S THE ONLY PLAYER TO HAVE DONE THIS!

CHAMPIONSHIPS

Pelé not only played in a different **era** than Messi, but also mostly on a different continent. With Santos, Pelé defeated the top teams in South America in the Copa Libertadores. This tournament began in 1960 and is compared to today's Champions League in Europe.

TWO-TIME COPA LIBERTADORES CHAMPION WITH SANTOS

TWO-TIME INTERCONTINENTAL CUP WINNER WITH SANTOS

PELÉ WON THE COPA LIBERTADORES AND THE INTERCONTINENTAL CUP IN THE SAME YEARS: 1962 AND 1963.

Messi played for Barcelona from 2004 to 2021. They won the Champions League and La Liga many times! Messi played for Paris Saint-Germain FC (PSG) in France from 2021 to 2023. He led his team to championships there as well.

FOUR-TIME CHAMPIONS LEAGUE WINNER WITH FC BARCELONA

TEN-TIME LA LIGA WINNER WITH FC BARCELONA

TWO-TIME LIGUE 1 CHAMPION WITH PSG

LIGUE 1 IS A TOP SOCCER LEAGUE IN FRANCE THAT PSG IS PART OF.

Did You Know?

The Intercontinental Cup had the winner of the Copa Libertadores face the winner of the European Cup (now the Champions League).

GOAL!

How many goals Pelé scored in his career isn't entirely clear. Pelé himself said he had over 1,200 career goals, a fact accepted by Guinness World Records. But this number includes goals scored in non-league games, youth games, and games against **amateur** teams.

PELÉ ALSO HOLDS THE RECORD FOR THE MOST HAT TRICKS OF ANY SOCCER PLAYER IN HISTORY.

BRAZIL NATIONAL TEAM'S ALL-TIME LEADING SCORER (77 GOALS)

GUINNESS WORLD RECORD HOLDER FOR MOST CAREER GOALS (1,279)

643 GOALS SCORED WITH SANTOS

Did You Know?

Today, the number of a player's total career goals comes from official, first-class games. For Pelé, that number would be about 778 at most.

As of mid-2025, Messi has scored more than 870 career goals. As he continues to play, this number will continue to increase. He holds the record for most career goals of an FC Barcelona player with 672!

MESSI'S CAREER GOALS TOTAL INCLUDES THOSE HE SCORED FOR FC BARCELONA AND PSG, AS WELL AS INTER MIAMI CF, THE TEAM HE PLAYS FOR IN U.S. MAJOR LEAGUE SOCCER (MLS). IT ALSO INCLUDES ALL THOSE HE HAS SCORED AS A MEMBER OF THE ARGENTINE NATIONAL TEAM.

ALL-TIME LEADING SCORER IN LA LIGA (474)

SECOND-HIGHEST NUMBER OF OFFICIAL CAREER GOALS IN SOCCER HISTORY

ALL-TIME LEADING SCORER FOR ARGENTINA'S NATIONAL TEAM

RECORD FOR MOST GOALS SCORED IN ONE YEAR (91 IN 2012)

Did You Know?

Messi and Cristiano Ronaldo are the only soccer players to have scored more than 800 official career goals. Ronaldo has scored more than 940!

HOW MANY GAMES?

The Guinness World Records reports that between September 1956 and October 1977, Pelé played in more than 1,300 games. This number includes friendlies and **exhibition** games. Pelé played more than 90 games for the Brazilian national team.

PELÉ PLAYED FOR THE NEW YORK COSMOS OF THE NORTH AMERICAN SOCCER LEAGUE FROM 1975 TO 1977. HE PLAYED IN 64 GAMES FOR THE COSMOS.

1,363 TOTAL CAREER GAMES

Did You Know?

A friendly is a soccer game between two teams that doesn't count toward league play. It's mostly for training.

As of mid-2025, Messi has played in more than 1,100 games. Since **professional** soccer games commonly last about 95 minutes, that means he has played more than 100,000 minutes of professional soccer!

MESSI HAS BEEN ON THE WINNING SIDE FAR MORE THAN THE LOSING SIDE THROUGHOUT HIS MANY GAMES.

779 OFFICIAL GAMES PLAYED WITH FC BARCELONA

63,614 MINUTES PLAYED WITH FC BARCELONA

Did You Know?

Professional soccer games are officially 90 minutes long. Extra time is added to account for any stops in play.

THE BALLON D'OR

Today, the Ballon d'Or is the prize given out each year to the best soccer players, male and female, in the world. Messi holds the record for the most Ballons d'Or awarded to a male player, having won the award in 2009, 2010, 2011, 2012, 2015, 2019, 2021, and 2023.

Pelé never won the Ballon d'Or. That's because until 1995, the prize could only be given to a player from Europe, and until 2007, only those playing for European teams could win it.

Did You Know?

The player who wins the Ballon d'Or is decided by a vote of **journalists** from around the world who cover soccer.

EIGHT-TIME BALLON D'OR WINNER

MESSI'S MANY BALLON D'OR WINS SHOW THAT HE HAS BEEN RECOGNIZED AROUND THE WORLD FOR HIS GREAT PLAY ON THE SOCCER FIELD.

WORLDWIDE GREATNESS

Even long after Pelé stopped playing soccer, he was honored as one of the best players of all time. *Sports Illustrated* named him third on its list of the greatest soccer players ever. As the accompanying entry said: "Pelé is important. The most important player of all time."

NAMED ATHLETE OF THE CENTURY BY THE INTERNATIONAL OLYMPIC COMMITTEE IN 1999

FIFA PLAYER OF THE CENTURY

ONE OF 100 MOST IMPORTANT PEOPLE OF THE 20TH CENTURY, ACCORDING TO *TIME*

THERE'S NO DOUBT THAT PELÉ'S AMAZING PLAY ON THE FIELD EARNED HIM THESE HONORS, AMONG OTHERS.

Sports Illustrated named Messi number one on its list of the greatest soccer players of all time. During his more than 20-year career, Messi has been honored many other times, including with the Presidential Medal of Freedom in 2025!

OLYMPIC GOLD MEDALIST (2008)

SEVEN-TIME LA LIGA PLAYER OF THE YEAR

FIVE-TIME EUROPEAN GOLDEN SHOE WINNER

BEST FIFA MEN'S PLAYER (2023)

MESSI WON THE GOLDEN SHOE AWARDS FOR SCORING THE MOST POINTS OF ANY PLAYER IN THE TOP SOCCER LEAGUES OF EUROPE.

U.S. IMPACT

Professional soccer wasn't popular in the United States in the 1970s. Pelé surprised fans by signing with the New York Cosmos in 1975. His presence boosted the top home game attendance from about 8,000 to over 70,000!

PELÉ WAS CHOSEN AS A NORTH AMERICAN SOCCER LEAGUE ALL-STAR IN ALL THREE OF HIS SEASONS WITH THE COSMOS.

Did You Know?

Pelé had **retired** from both Santos and the Brazilian national team before playing in North America.

When Messi's contract with PSG ran out, he thought about going back to FC Barcelona. Instead, he began playing for Inter Miami CF in 2023. His arrival increased game attendance, ticket prices, and TV viewers.

ONE OF THE INTER MIAMI OWNER'S LONG-TERM GOALS WAS TO BRING MESSI TO MIAMI. HE STARTED WORKING ON IT IN 2018!

REACHING OUT

Both Pelé and Messi have proven their greatness off the field as well. Pelé **supported** many causes during his life. In 2018, the Pelé **Foundation** was established. Its main goal was to fight childhood **poverty**.

Messi started the Leo Messi Foundation in 2007. It focuses on bettering health care, education, and access to sports for children and teenagers. In addition, he began working with UNICEF, a group that helps children around the world, in 2010.

Did You Know?

Pelé died on December 29, 2022. His foundation continues to work to make the world a better place in his name.

WHAT DO YOU THINK? WHO'S THE GREATEST—PELÉ OR MESSI?

GLOSSARY

amateur: Someone who does something without pay.

career: The job someone chooses to do for a long time.

era: A period of time.

exhibition: A public showing of something.

foundation: A not-for-profit organization provided with funds to support charitable works.

journalist: A person who reports on world happenings.

league: A group of sports teams that face each other.

poverty: The state of being poor.

professional: Earning money from an activity that many people do for fun.

retire: To leave a job.

support: To hold up and help.

tournament: A series of contests testing the skill of many athletes in the same sport.

FOR MORE INFORMATION

BOOKS

Lewis, Leigh. *Lionel Messi*. Mankato, MN: Amicus Learning, 2026.

Streissguth, Thomas. *Soccer Greats: The Best of All Time*. San Diego, CA: ReferencePoint Press, Inc., 2026.

WEBSITES

Lionel Messi's Official Website
messi.com/en/
Follow what Messi is up to here.

Pelé Foundation
www.pele10.org/home
Learn more about the Pelé Foundation.

Publisher's note to educators and parents: Our editors have carefully reviewed these websites to ensure that they are suitable for students. Many websites change frequently, however, and we cannot guarantee that a site's future contents will continue to meet our high standards of quality and educational value. Be advised that students should be closely supervised whenever they access the internet.

INDEX